D0919871

Help America Heal

A story of hope for young people

By Peggy A. Rothbaum, Ph.D., LLC

drpeggyrothbaum.com

Printed in the U.S.A.

Help America Heal: A story of hope for young people by Peggy A. Rothbaum, Ph.D., LLC

Layout and digital design by M. Kovalyov happyfamilyart.com

ISBN 978-0-9883592-1-5

drpeggyrothbaum.com

Beloved World LLC
232 Saint Paul Street
Westfield, NJ 07090
belovedworldllc@gmail.com

Dedication

This book is dedicated to our beloved world.

Our country
is hurting.

People are
upset.

This is scary and upsetting for kids.

People seem angry.

Lots of them are saying mean stuff to each other.

"I don't like you."

"YOU ARE STUPID."

"You are not good enough to be an American."

"You are lazy."

"You are taking stuff that should be mine."

What is happening in America?

Why are so many people angry, upset, and sad?

America should not be like this! The United States of America is supposed to have liberty and justice for all!

I pledge allegiance to the flag of the United States of America, and to the republic for which it stands, one nation under God, indivisible, with liberty and justice for all.

In America's history, we haven't always treated everyone right.

We had slaves: 1654 - 1865.

We took land from the Native Americans: Trail of Tears, 1839-1939.

We treated the Japanese people wrongly: Internment of Japanese Americans, 1942-1945.

We have a lot of hatred in America.

Some people hate each other for really dumb reasons.

Your skin color is not like mine.

You speak a different language.

You like people who are the same sex as you.

You think different stuff is important than what I think.

Your God is not the same as my God.

Your family comes from a different country.

We have some problems too.

Not enough jobs.

Too many people who get upset that everyone is not the same.

People from other countries want to come here.

TOO MANY POOR PEOPLE.

NOT ENOUGH DOCTORS.

People losing their jobs.

People not taking care of the earth.

People being mean to animals.

Too many guns.

Our problems in
America scare people
and make them upset.

Think about it. What do you want to do when you are scared or upset?

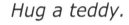

Hug a teddy.

Try to keep everything the same.

Sit in a corner and cry.

Stay with people who comfort you.

Find people who understand how you feel.

Find people like you.

That's okay, but another way not to be afraid is to learn new ideas and try to understand how different people think and feel.

Then we don't have to be so afraid.

You are like me even though your
skin is a different color.

And you have a different God.

And you speak a different language.

You have only one parent,
but you are so loved!

You are poor, but you try hard.

You try to be fair and nice to other kids.

This could help
America to heal!

What else can we do to help
America heal?

We can talk to other people
about what we know about
new ideas and different
people.

We can think and learn more
about ourselves,
how we feel, and how we treat
others.

We can be
kind.

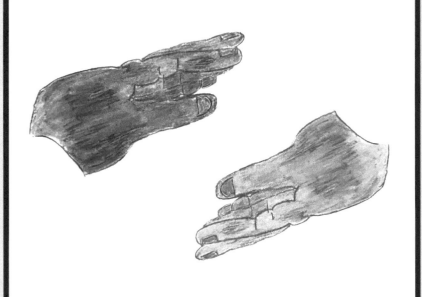

When times are hard, we can help each other.

We can write and make art.

We can take care of the earth.

We can take care of our air, water, and land. We can do community projects.

YES   NO

We can take care of the birds, bugs, reptiles, fish, butterflies, bees, and animals.

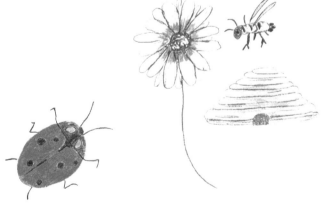

Elephants need our protection. They are very intelligent. They live in families and also form their own communities.

Scientists have shown that elephants become sad when they are forced to live alone or to give rides.

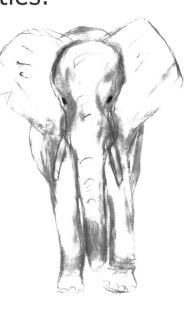

We need to protect apes and their habitat.

Apes are very smart. Apes have relationships with other apes.

It is not good for them to be caged.

We need to protect dolphins too. Dolphins are very smart. They communicate with each other in different ways.

They belong swimming free, not in captivity or doing tricks.

Whales need our help too.
They are intelligent. They
speak and sing. Whales
teach each other and make
plans together.

Whales grieve and are sad
sometimes. They need to
swim free.

We can help whales, dolphins, elephants, and apes by setting them free, keeping them safe, and helping them to live in ways that are best for them.

Sometimes we need to rescue animals.

Woof-Meow   *Express*

Let's rescue them all!

We are all connected.

Because we all make a
difference.

There are so many
things we can do to
help America heal!

We cannot give up! We must keep trying to heal America!

Dr. Peggy Rothbaum (drpeggyrothbaum.com) is a psychologist, writer, researcher, and consultant in Westfield, New Jersey. She also does community service, creates art, and passionately advocates for animals. Her main mission in life is to help make the world a better place. Her first co-authored picture book is Taking Care of Little Snoogie: A Story About Pet Loss for Adults.

CPSIA information can be obtained
at www.ICGtesting.com
Printed in the USA
BVHW021951180721
612103BV00001B/3